Violin

String Time Starters

21 pieces for flexible ensemble

Kathy and David Blackwell

Illustrations by Martin Remphry

Full performances and backing tracks for all pieces are available to download from the *String Time Starters* Companion Website: www.oup.co.uk/companion/stringtimestarters.

MUSIC DEPARTMENT

OXFORD
UNIVERSITY PRESS

Just for Starters: warm ups

1. Hill and gully rider

Jamaican trad.
arr. KB & DB

Let's all play the D string, I can play D!

I can play D!

2. Aiken drum

Scottish trad.
arr. KB & DB

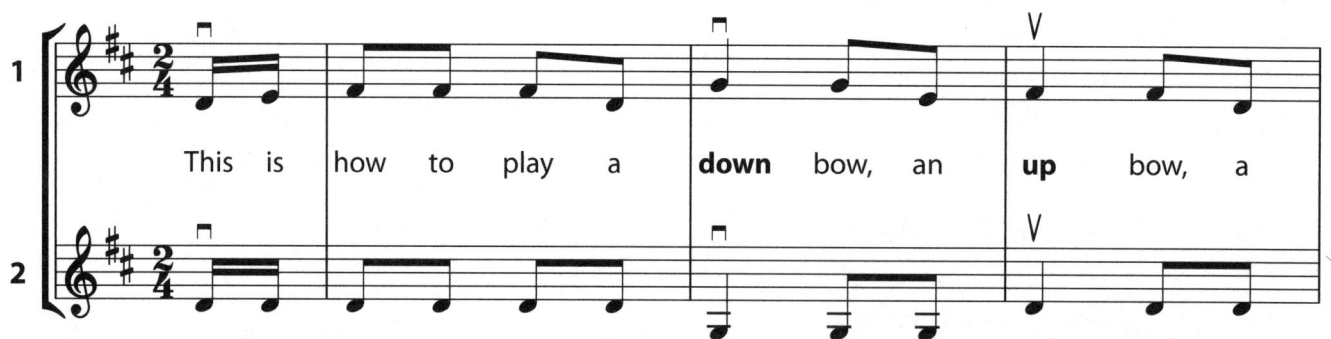

This is how to play a **down** bow, an **up** bow, a

down bow, this is how to play a **down** bow, in the orch-es-tra.

Printed in Great Britain

OXFORD UNIVERSITY PRESS, MUSIC DEPARTMENT, GREAT CLARENDON STREET, OXFORD OX2 6DP

3. Pizzicato polka

Johann Strauss II (1825–99)
arr. KB & DB

4. Arpeggio can-can

Jacques Offenbach (1819–80)
arr. KB & DB

5. Wake up! (round and ostinato)

KB & DB

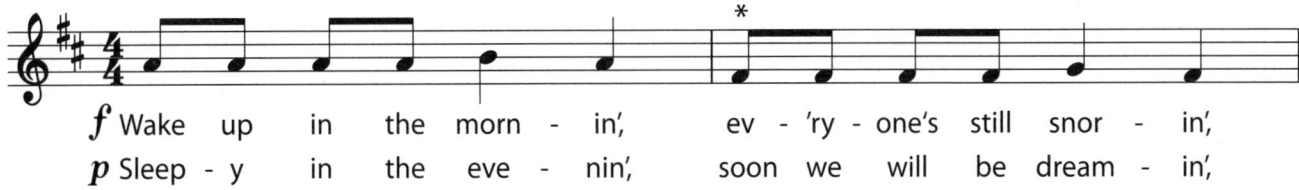

f Wake up in the morn - in', ev - 'ry - one's still snor - in',
p Sleep - y in the eve - nin', soon we will be dream - in',

get 'em out of bed with a wake up shout. Hey!
time to go to bed with a lul - la - by. Shh!

New parts enter at ∗. The last two bars can also be played as an ostinato.

1. Show time!

KB & DB

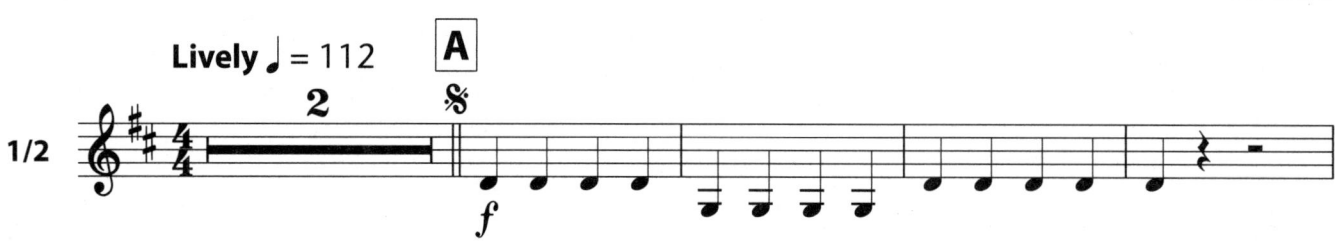

2. Sword dance

Thoinot Arbeau (1520–95)
arr. KB & DB

3. Let's play a rag

KB & DB

4. Midnight feast

KB & DB

Creepily ♩ = 60

Creep - ing round at mid - night just like a hun - gry beast, Look - ing for some food that - 'll make a mid - night feast. Choc - 'late cake and le - mon - ade make a tast - y snack, Shh! I hear some foot - steps, time to tip - toe back! Tip - toe, tip - toe, tip - toe, tip - toe. Yum!

5. Chicken on a fencepost

American trad.
arr. KB & DB

6. Mellow-D

KB & DB

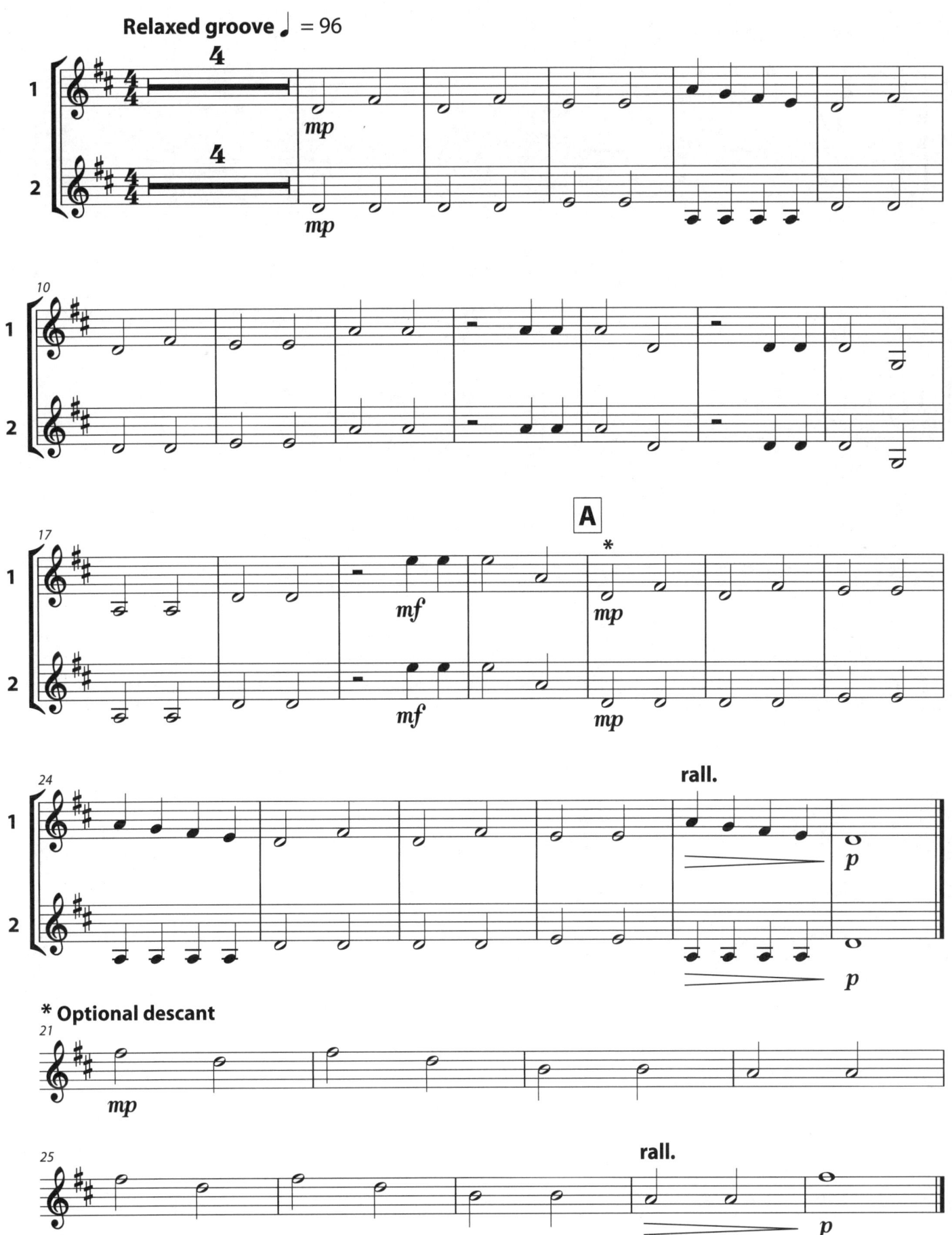

* Optional descant

7. Take your partners

KB & DB

8. Daydream

KB & DB

Gently ♩ = 108

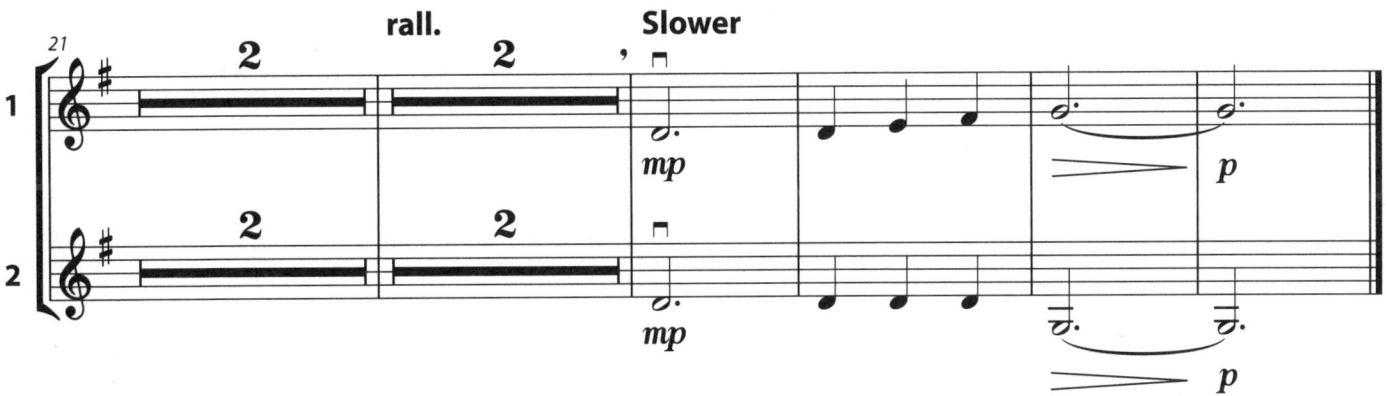

9. Take the D train

KB & DB

1st time: Slow ♩ = 92
2nd time: Fast! ♩ = 116

1st time: gradually get faster

Give the effect of a train gradually gathering speed then travelling at a fast pace.

10. Three-legged race

KB & DB

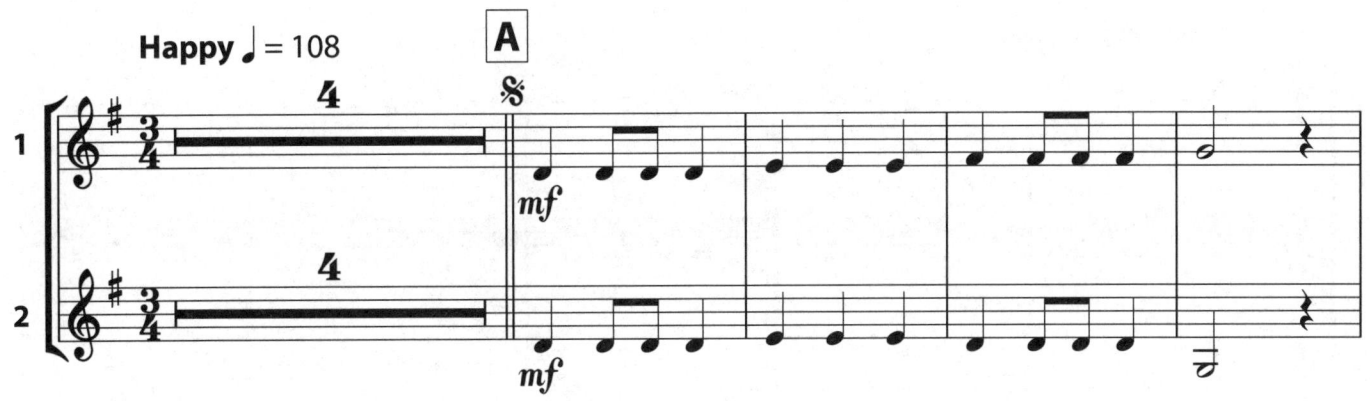

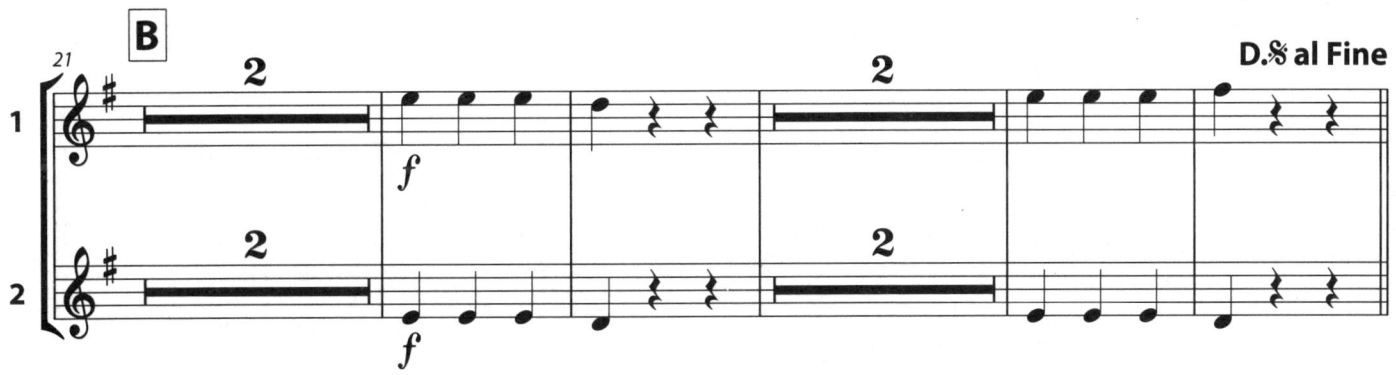

11. Boogie

KB & DB

12. Time to tango

KB & DB

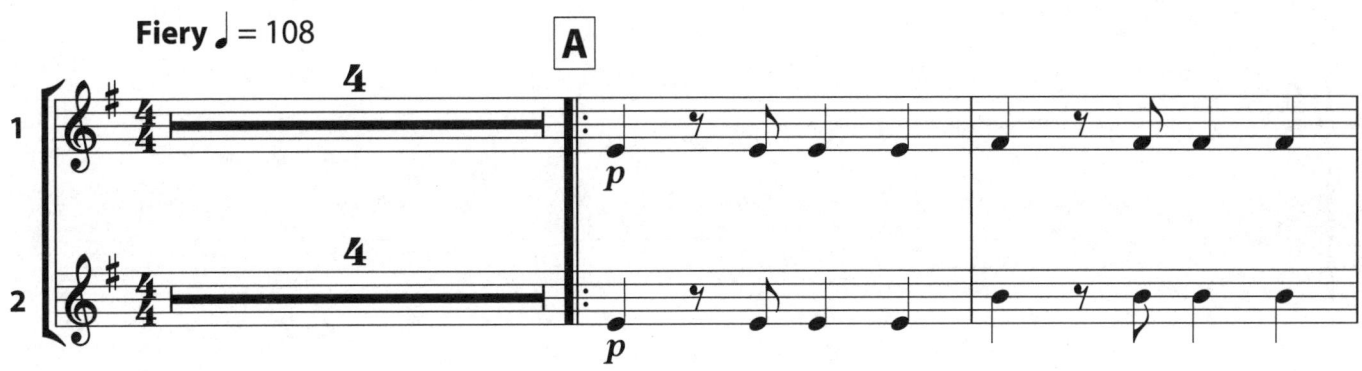

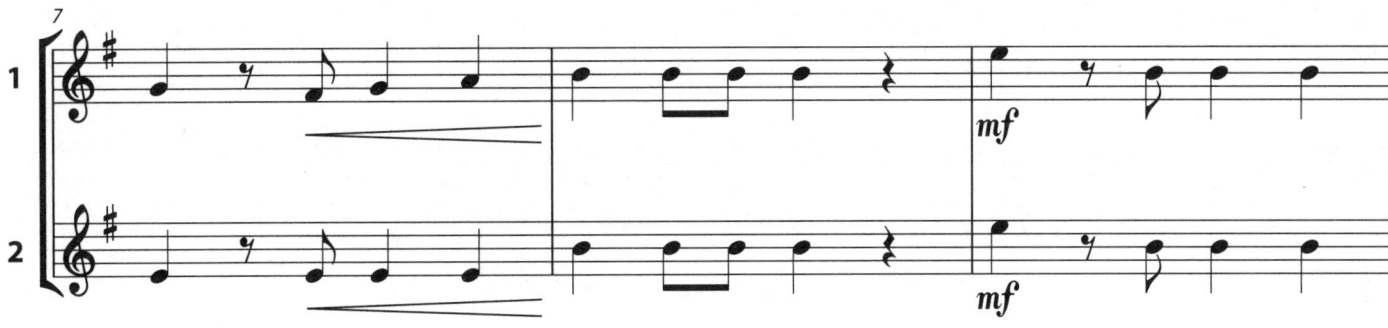

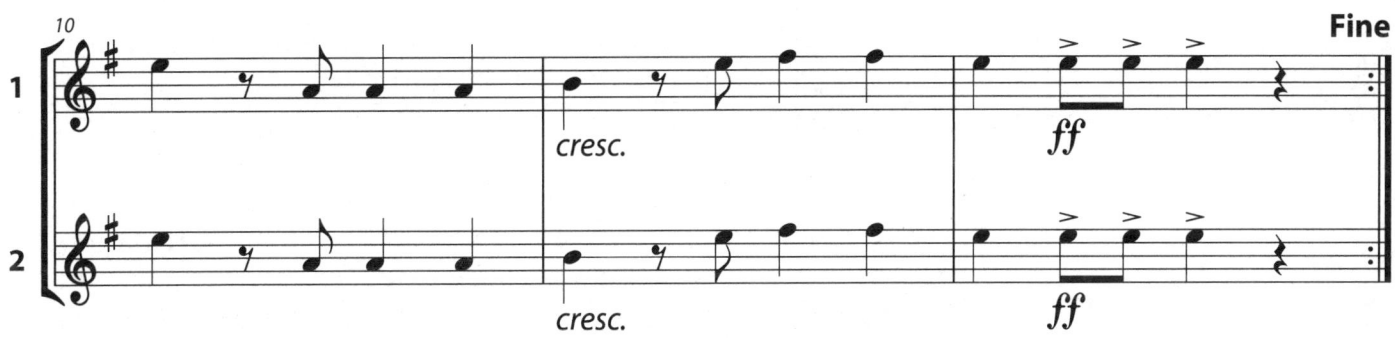

13. Let's rock!

KB & DB

14. Circus tricks

KB & DB

15. Ode to Joy

Ludwig van Beethoven (1770–1827)
arr. KB & DB

Joyfully ♩ = 100

16. Skye boat song

Scottish trad.
arr. KB & DB

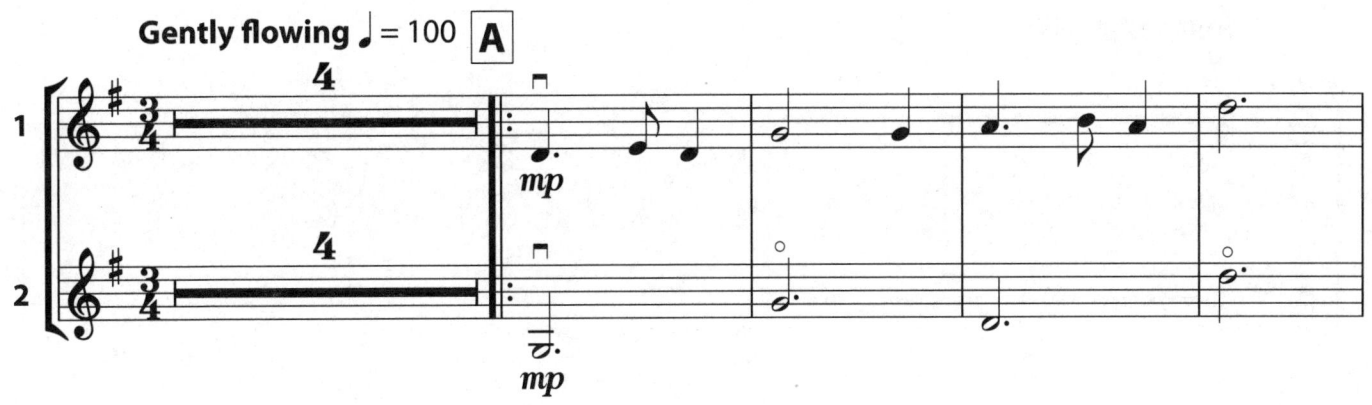

(rall. and pause **2nd time** only)

17. Mary had a baby

American trad.
arr. KB & DB

Relaxed ♩ = 76

1 — Ma - ry had a ba - by, Yes, Lord!_

Ma - ry had a ba - by, Yes, my Lord! Ma - ry had a ba - by,

Yes, Lord! Peo - ple keep a - com - in', and the train done gone!

18. Jingle, bells

J. Pierpont (1822–93)
arr. KB & DB

Cheerfully ♩ = 80

Jin - gle, bells, jin - gle, bells, jin - gle all the

way; Oh, what fun it is to ride in a one - horse o - pen

sleigh!___ Jin - gle, bells, jin - gle, bells, jin - gle all the way;

Oh, what fun it is to ride in a one - horse o - pen sleigh!

19. Canoe song

Native American Indian song
arr. KB & DB

Strongly ♩ = 80

My pad - dle's keen and bright, flash - ing with

sil - ver. Fol - low the wild goose flight, dip, dip and swing.

A

(stamp)   (stamp)   (stamp,

(stamp)   (stamp)   (stamp,

p   *cresc.*   *mf*

B *★ f*

stamp!)

stamp!)   My pad - dle's keen and bright, flash-ing with sil - ver. Fol - low the

f

(stamp, stamp!)

wild goose flight, dip, dip and swing.   **2**   (stamp, stamp!)

★ Optional descant

B   (stamp, stamp!)   **2**

f

20. G-force blues

KB & DB

With a heavy beat ♩ = 112

21. Hush, little baby

American trad.
arr. KB & DB